ISBN: 978-1-7332672-7-4 (paperback)

eBook available for immediate download (free on Amazon with kindle unlimited plan)

Moore Substance Publishing
Original publication 2020

Edited by Marilyn Beach

Table of Contents

Introduction

According to the grace of God which was given to me, as a wise master builder I have laid the foundation, and another builds on it. But let each one take heed how he builds on it. For no other foundation can anyone lay than that which is laid, which is Jesus Christ.

I Corinthians 3:10-11 NKJV

The foundation of this devotional is Jesus Christ. To fully receive what's meant for you, be sure to pray before you read, and then keep Him in mind when living and sharing it.

One

In the beginning God created the heaven and the earth. And the earth was without form, and void; and darkness was upon the face of the deep. And the Spirit of God moved upon the face of the waters. And God said, Let there be light: and there was light. And God saw the light, that it was good: and God divided the light from the darkness. And God called the light Day, and the darkness he called Night. And the evening and the morning were the first day.

Genesis 1:1-5 KJV

And God saw every thing that he had made, and, behold, it was very good. And the evening and the morning were the sixth day.
Thus the heavens and the earth were finished, and all the host of them. And on the seventh day God ended his work which he had made; and he rested on the seventh day from all his work which he had made. And God blessed the seventh day, and sanctified it: because that in it

he had rested from all his work which God
created and made.

Genesis 1:31 and 2:1-3 KJV

Let's look at three main things that we can learn
from these scriptures and a few more concerning
creation.

(1) When it came to creation, God didn't just
"rush" or do everything at once, on the same
day. Clearly, He had the power to. He was more
than likely setting a blueprint for us. You may be
familiar with the locution, "Rome wasn't built in
a day" and the word outlines that heavens and
earth weren't either. So, take your time, enjoy
the process. Don't scurry greatness. Don't rush
your finances, job, or relationships. Don't be
anxious to be older, taller, faster or richer. If our
omnipotent and omniscient Father didn't hasten
things, neither should we. Value the journey,
savor your daily accomplishments, and give
thanks to God along the way.

Genesis 1:11-12 KJV *And God said, Let the earth bring forth grass, the herb yielding seed, and the fruit tree yielding fruit after his kind, whose seed is in itself, upon the earth: and it was so. And the earth brought forth grass, and herb yielding seed after his kind, and the tree yielding fruit, whose seed was in itself, after his kind: and God saw that it was good.*

Genesis 1:26-27 KJV *And God said, Let us make man in our image, after our likeness: and let them have dominion over the fish of the sea, and over the fowl of the air, and over the cattle, and over all the earth, and over every creeping thing that creepeth upon the earth. So God created man in his own image, in the image of God created he him; male and female created he them.*

(2) He's a God of order. He created everything else, including food to eat, and then He created man, whom He gave dominion over everything. He understood that it would've been backwards to create man but have neither a suitable place

for him to dwell and manage nor even food for
him to consume.

*And the Lord God took the man, and put him
into the garden of Eden to dress it and to keep it.*

Genesis 2:15 KJV

(3) He already had a plan in place to maintain
what He created. That means He truly thought it
all out. According to Genesis 1:26-27, we were
created in their image (Father, Son and Spirit),
so we should follow God's lead and think things
through before we say, do or build something.
Part of our thinking/planning process, is seeking
Him first, making sure our plans line up with His
will. *A man's heart deviseth his way: but the
Lord directeth his steps.* Proverbs☐ 16:9☐ KJV

Two

And the Lord God formed man of the dust of the ground, and breathed into his nostrils the breath of life; and man became a living soul.

Genesis 2:7 KJV

In the sweat of thy face shalt thou eat bread, till thou return unto the ground; for out of it wast thou taken: for dust thou art, and unto dust shalt thou return.

Genesis 3:19 KJV

A great way to stay humble is by remembering that we didn't create ourselves. We started from the bottom (shout out to Aubrey Graham), literally. Our Creator had and still has the ability: to take something dirty and make it whole, to form greatness out of rudimentary elements, and to give prominence to what was originally insignificant. Yes, God can uplift, sanctify, and give confidence to what others used to walk all over. Never downplay what you consider meaningless. With the help of God, it can become AMAZING.

Three

Those who control their tongue will have a long life; opening your mouth can ruin everything.

Proverbs 13:3 NLT

The tongue can bring death or life; those who love to talk will reap the consequences.

Proverbs 18:21 NLT

Compared to the entire body, the tongue is but a tiny portion. That said, it's no small task in trying to control it (see James 3:1-12). People disciplined in controlling what they communicate -verbally, typed or handwritten- will reap MAJOR benefits throughout their lives. Controlling what you say is a skill that must be prayed about, cultivated, and constantly in the forefront of your mind. It's something that isn't mastered overnight or completed after one conversation. Even though we have the liberties to say many things (including things that may be true), it doesn't mean that they NEED to be said. James 1:19 tells us to be swift to hear and SLOW to speak. We gain more by listening. If we're quick to cut someone off who's talking, we may miss out on important things, and even hamper or deaden the growth of that relationship. Also, saying any and everything on our minds or how we're currently feeling can ruin communication and authentic communication is VITAL to any relationship. I don't know anyone who's never said something that he/she later didn't regret or wish it would've been worded differently. Let's be mindful of what's on the tip of our tongues before we release it into an irretrievable atmosphere. A "speech filter" can be your best friend, because what you say can have a lasting effect, good or bad. I've realized that simply being quiet and listening can have the loudest impact on others.

Four

A soft answer turneth away wrath: but grievous words stir up anger.

Proverbs 15:1 KJV

Let's look at two examples of how this proverb played out in real life, in hopes that you'll apply it to your everyday interactions.

(1) *Then He came to Simon Peter. And Peter said to Him, "Lord, are You washing my feet?" Jesus answered and said to him, "What I am doing you do not understand now, but you will know after this." Peter said to Him, "You shall never wash my feet!" Jesus answered him, "If I do not wash you, you have no part with Me." Simon Peter said to Him, "Lord, not my feet only, but also my hands and my head!" Jesus said to him, "He who is bathed needs only to wash his feet, but is completely clean; and you are clean, but not all of you." John 13:6-10 NKJV*

After Peter told Jesus what He would NEVER do, God had the right to, as the sayings goes, "read him his rights" or "undress him." In front of everyone. But instead of escalating the situation and beating him over the head with His authority, He gave a soft reply. Even when Peter followed with what he exclaimed the Master would never do, with instructions on what He should do instead, Jesus was still calm, unagitated and patient as He replied in love.

(2) *Again, a second time, He went away and prayed, saying, "O My Father, if this cup cannot pass away from Me unless I drink it, Your will be done." And He came and found them asleep again, for their eyes were heavy. So He left them, went away again, and prayed the third time, saying the same words. Then He came to His disciples and said to them, "Are you still sleeping and resting? Behold, the hour is at hand, and the Son of Man is being*

betrayed into the hands of sinners. Rise, let us be going. See, My betrayer is at hand." Matthew 26:42-46 NKJV

This comes on the heels of Peter swearing that even if everyone else denies Him, he never will (verses 31-35). As well as, Jesus finding Peter, James and John asleep the first time He came back from praying (verses 36-41). Even with all of that having transpired AND Jesus about to be betrayed, brutally beaten, and hung on the cross to die, He still didn't raise his voice, belittle them, or use grievous words. If at one of, if not THE most trying time of His life, Jesus was still gentle and loving in how he spoke and dealt with others, we should make up our minds to do the same, with the help of the Holy Spirit.

Five

Command those who are rich in this present age not to be haughty, nor to trust in uncertain riches but in the living God, who gives us richly all things to enjoy.

1 Timothy 6:17 NKJV

The Covid-19 pandemic was eye-opening to some and a reminder to others, that you can't trust in uncertain riches. Government agencies, movie theaters, malls, manufacturers, barbershops, beauty shops, nail shops, restaurants, clubs, and even churches were forced to close their doors to the public and re-evaluate how they conduct day to day business. Needless to say, it cost a lot of people money and forced them to realize how true this Word is. Any time you put your trust in anything outside of God, to provide for your resources, you will be disappointed. Nothing outside of

God is reliable, guaranteed or lasting. Don't put your trust or dependence in a job or resource; instead, always have faith and trust in THE Source, Who provides all of your needs, talents and resources.

Six

Understand this, my dear brothers and sisters: You must all be quick to listen, slow to speak, and slow to get angry.

James 1:19 NLT

God speaks to us in many different ways. His word, His ordained ministers, the Holy Spirit, visions, dreams, and many more. But a lot of times we're too busy telling Him what we need and want, constantly speaking to and at Him. Instead of being still, meditating on His word (what He's saying to you through the scriptures) and applying it. We should all be eager and quick to listen to what the Creator, Master, and all-knowing God of the universe has to say to us. Instead, we are so quick to speak or talk about the basic things that our father already knows we need and readily supplies (see Matthew 6:25-34). Not to mention we shouldn't be so quick to get angry. Especially when we can't see the entire or bigger picture. So, whether you lose your job, get injured, have your heart broken, get low on finances, struggle with a decision, etc., it'd be wiser to listen to what God, the one who knows the beginning and end, is saying to you instead of getting angry and doing all the talking.

Seven

Don't be selfish; don't try to impress others. Be humble, thinking of others as better than yourselves. Don't look out only for your own interests, but take an interest in others, too.

Philippians 2:3-4 NLT

If you apply this verse to your daily life, it will strengthen your relationship with others. If you're married and you follow this word, you'll not only be obedient to the Lord, but you'll be doing your part in cultivating a potent covenant relationship. Selfishness and conceit can ruin any relationship and drain those around you. On the other hand, when you're humble, not making everything about yourself, but also taking genuine interest in what others desire and want, you position yourself to reap amazing benefits as well. It also gives you a chance to expand your knowledge, while giving you a better understanding.

Eight

Wickedness never brings stability, but the godly have deep roots.

Proverbs 12:3 NLT

Have you ever seen those television shows (<u>Power</u>, <u>Ozark</u>, <u>The Chi</u>) where wicked people are always facing some bizarre challenge every other day of their lives? They never truly have any joy, peace or stability? That's Hollywood mimicking real life. We can't live morally dysfunctional lives and expect things to be kosher. No one is immune to trials or unforeseen situations, but when we make godly choices, and delight in the law of the Lord, our roots will be as deep as a tree planted near a body of water, whose roots go down deep, so when the harsh weather hits, we will still be fruitful and prosperous, unlike the ungodly. Read the first Psalm for confirmation.

Nine

A wise child accepts a parent's discipline; a mocker refuses to listen to correction.

Proverbs 13:1 NLT

Even if your parents' ways aren't the wisest, it would be foolish to buck against the authority and hands that feed, clothe, house and provide for you. Being respectful, even when you don't agree with your guardians, and following the rules of the house (home, work, school, job, etc.) is a prudent way of life. Scoffing at the parental authority that God has placed you under will cripple you in more areas than you realize and leave you with a warped sense of reality, when it comes to future authority figures that God has ordained to help you grow, mature and thrive.

Ten

So teach us to number our days, that we may apply our hearts unto wisdom.

Psalms 90:12 KJV

Lord, remind me how brief my time on earth will be. Remind me that my days are numbered— how fleeting my life is.

Psalms 39:4 NLT

How short life is will eventually enter our thoughts, no matter what the prompt: a reminder from God like the Psalmist, weekly reflection on it ourselves, or the loss of someone else's life. When it does, it's up to us to be smarter about how we live and use our time on earth. Death is inevitable or at least the quality of life that you currently have. Your transition may be different (a paralyzing accident, debilitating disease, terminal illness, well-advanced age or death) but the final conclusion will be the same, if the rapture tarries. You never know when life as you know it will cease to exist. Therefore, it's up to you to prioritize your God-granted time in the most efficient ways possible.

Eleven

Don't let the excitement of youth cause you to forget your Creator. Honor him in your youth before you grow old and say, "Life is not pleasant anymore."

Ecclesiastes 12:1 NLT

Don't wait until you're old and doddery to try and worship and serve the Lord wholeheartedly. You should recognize and honor God when things are going great and you're feeling invincible, not just when you're in need or unable to do the things you used to enjoy.

Twelve

*Because you disdained all my counsel, And
would have none of my rebuke, I also will laugh
at your calamity; I will mock when your terror
comes, When your terror comes like a storm,
And your destruction comes like a whirlwind,
When distress and anguish come upon you.
Then they will call on me, but I will not answer;
They will seek me diligently, but they will not
find me. Because they hated knowledge and did
not choose the fear of the LORD, They would
have none of my counsel And despised my every
rebuke. Therefore they shall eat the fruit of their
own way, And be filled to the full with their own
fancies.*

Proverbs 1:25-31 NKJV

When you have a lack of respect for the word of
God and even despise it, what would make you
think that when you call out to God (even
atheist, have been known to do this) in your

most hopeless and destressing moments, that He would do whatever you desired? He'll allow you to reap the fruit from the seeds you've planted, watered and cultivated over the years. In other words, lie in the bed that you repeatedly and purposely made on your own. If you continuously refuse to acknowledge God, He'll eventually leave you to your own mess and let you wallow in it. And once He does that, good luck trying to clean it up on your own.

And even as they did not like to retain God in their knowledge, God gave them over to a debased mind, to do those things which are not fitting;
Romans 1:28 NKJV

Thirteen

And don't forget Sodom and Gomorrah and their neighboring towns, which were filled with immorality and every kind of sexual perversion. Those cities were destroyed by fire and serve as a warning of the eternal fire of God's judgment.

Jude 1:7 NLT

It would be unusually rare for your vehicle to have an engine issue that prevented you from driving it, without the warning light coming on and sometimes staying on for a prolonged period. Ignoring the warning light on your ride until things start smoking, clunking sounds come from under the hood, or power is lost, wouldn't be the best way to rectify the issue. At the very least, you should get a diagnostic done and find out what it would cost to get things back right. Verses five and six also serve as a warning (*But I want to remind you, though you once knew this, that the Lord, having saved the people out of the land of Egypt, afterward destroyed those who did not believe. And the angels who did not keep their proper domain, but left their own abode, He has reserved in everlasting chains under darkness for the judgment of the great day;* Jude 1:5-6 NKJV.) There are many other places throughout scripture, where God warns and tries to save us from going down similar unbefitting paths as believers. He'll even warn you through messages, other people, or by speaking to your conscious via His Holy Spirit. We should never let things get so out of control that we break down and have to be "towed" away. Don't ignore what God is telling you.

Fourteen

Be not afraid of sudden fear, neither of the desolation of the wicked, when it cometh.

Proverbs 3:25 KJV

Have not I commanded thee? Be strong and of a good courage; be not afraid, neither be thou dismayed: for the Lord thy God is with thee whithersoever thou goest.

Joshua 1:9 KJV

"Fear," "do not fear," "don't be afraid," or similar translations are mentioned in the Bible almost FOUR HUNDRED times. Clearly God knew that we would have an issue with fear and being afraid. He encourages and reassures us that all the security and safety we need is found in Him. We don't have to search anywhere else, ask for advice from unequipped and overly opinionated people on social media, or from our favorite carnal talk show host. Don't let fear push you away from God or drive a wedge between you and the faith you have in Him. Instead, use any sudden fear that you face to your advantage and for your good. Let it move you ever closer to God. When that starts to happen, even the enemy will hate when you become afraid, knowing it will only strengthen your relationship with your loving Creator.

Fifteen

And when the woman saw that the tree was good for food, and that it was pleasant to the eyes, and a tree to be desired to make one wise, she took of the fruit thereof, and did eat, and gave also unto her husband with her; and he did eat.

Genesis 3:6 KJV

When Eve ate and then gave it to her husband who was with her, I wonder if he felt pressured to partake in it. The serpent said it was good and Eve ate, so maybe he didn't want to be the odd man out. Perhaps he doubted God's word - that they would die - since Eve didn't immediately drop dead. Let's be real- had Eve died on the spot, I doubt Adam would've picked up the fruit that rolled out of her hand as she hit the ground and eaten as well. It's dangerous to second guess God's Word, when what you see, doesn't line up with His Word or promises.

Could it be that he wanted to please his wife or keep the peace? I'm sure if he had reprimanded her for going against God's command, especially in front of "company," that there could have been some backlash or tension. Or, was it that he thought he'd miss out on something she had gained or experienced, if he didn't join in? We may never know what he was thinking in that moment. But we do know the consequences and results that followed (if you're not familiar with what happened, keep reading after verse six) due to him following his wife's lead, instead of what he knew that God had commanded. I pray that you won't succumb to peer pressure, your own lustful desires, fear of being an outcast, or temptation from the enemy, when faced with decisions on whether to follow what you know God has directed or do your own thing.

Sixteen

Now the serpent was more subtil than any beast of the field which the Lord God had made. And he said unto the woman, Yea, hath God said, Ye shall not eat of every tree of the garden? And the woman said unto the serpent, We may eat of the fruit of the trees of the garden: But of the fruit of the tree which is in the midst of the garden, God hath said, Ye shall not eat of it, neither shall ye touch it, lest ye die. And the serpent said unto the woman, Ye shall not surely die: For God doth know that in the day ye eat thereof, then your eyes shall be opened, and ye shall be as gods, knowing good and evil.

Genesis 3:1-5 KJV

Like all of the dilemmas we face, God has the answers. We simply have to seek His wisdom and way. The same is true for Eve's situation. She was familiar with the word that God had passed down through Adam about the tree of the knowledge of good and evil. She had also experienced God's presence and had a relationship with Him. So, when the serpent told her something that was contrary to God's word, why didn't she simply ask God? There will always be times when we're confused or second guess what we know is true. In those moments and any other, we should seek God for clarity and truth. He is not the God of confusion ((see 1 Corinthians 14:33 KJV) and He's never far from us or hard to reach, especially when you talk with Him daily. God will always confirm His Word; all you have to do is ask Him.

Seventeen

And the LORD said to Satan, "Behold, all that he has is in your power; only do not lay a hand on his person." So Satan went out from the presence of the LORD.

Job 1:12 NKJV

It's comforting to know that the thief, who wants to kill, steal, and destroy, can't just do any and everything that he desires. He can't wreak havoc on the world or in your individual life unless he's given permission to (Because of choices you've made, authority you've given over, God permits it to make you stronger or as a part of Him chastening you). Thank your omnipotent God for His love and protective hedge around you (see Job 1:9-10).

Eighteen

Thus Saul saw and knew that the LORD was with David, and that Michal, Saul's daughter, loved him; and Saul was still more afraid of David. So Saul became David's enemy continually.

I Samuel 18:28-29 NKJV

Jealousy and fear can lead you to doing some ungodly things, including lies, hate and murder. (Read verses 1-21 of how Saul became jealous and really wanted him dead.) If you ever feel jealousy coming on, check yourself and those emotions. Find the root cause and then correct it. Most of the time it won't change without God's help. Never let the fear of someone else doing better than you, taking "your spot" or receiving adulation, drive you to hatred, envy or murder. Why hate because God is with someone? Why be mad because He has elevated or prompted them? God knows best.

Nineteen

Saul took him that day, and would not let him go home to his father's house anymore. Then Jonathan and David made a covenant, because he loved him as his own soul. And Jonathan took off the robe that was on him and gave it to David, with his armor, even to his sword and his bow and his belt.

I Samuel 18:2-4 NKJV

Everyone wants or could use a Jonathan but who is willing to be a Jonathan? To be a Jonathan, you must sacrifice. Being a Jonathan is impossible without maturity. To be a Jonathan, you must have love instead of bitterness and jealousy. To be a Jonathan you have to be selflessness. After all, he was the heir to the kingdom. Do you realize ALL that he stood to inherit as the king? If not, research what Saul, David and Solomon had. We're talking luxury upon lavishness. Servants, fame, riches, legacy, power, the palace, the best choices of his wants and more. If he were worldly and all about his own gain, he would've been threatened by David and possibly tried to take him out like his father, King Saul. Instead, Jonathan embodied Philippians 2:3-4 NKJV, *Let nothing be done through selfish ambition or conceit, but in lowliness of mind let each esteem others better than himself. Let each of you look out not only for his own interests, but also for the interests of others.*

Twenty

Love is patient and kind. Love is not jealous or boastful or proud or rude. It does not demand its own way. It is not irritable, and it keeps no record of being wronged.

1 Corinthians 13:5 NLT

Verse five reminds us that real love doesn't DEMAND its own way. It isn't self-seeking. It doesn't insist that everything must go according to its desires. If you say you love someone, but everything has to be your way or not at all, that's not authentic love. If you're not happy or satisfied unless you get your way with someone, you don't really love that person. If all you think about is how you can be happy and pleased, or how someone can benefit you, then you don't really love them; you just love and are consumed with yourself.

Twenty-One

Always be humble and gentle. Be patient with each other, making allowance for each other's faults because of your love.

Ephesians 4:2 NLT

This verse lives in the forefront of my mind and affects how I treat and interact with people. Knowing that I make mistakes throughout the week, it would be foolish of me to think that others don't or won't. I don't care who you are, you will make mistakes and need others' forgiveness and grace. Some mistakes are small and others are big, but we all make them. Realizing this, I'm never surprised or caught off guard by my errors or someone else's. I have already done like the Word says and given them room to mess up. And when they do, I don't attack or crucify them. My love for them outweighs their faults. My understanding, that I'm just as flawed and capable of falling or failing as the next person, keeps me humble and allows me to deal with them as gently as I would want someone to handle me when I'm wrong or out of line. Lastly, God has been and still is, beyond patient with me, so the least I can do is extend an abundant amount of that patience to others. With the help of the Holy Spirit and a desire to do so, we all can follow and implement this Word in our daily walk.

Twenty-two

Wherefore, my beloved brethren, let every man be swift to hear, slow to speak, slow to wrath:

James 1:19 KJV

I include this verse in my daily prayers: asking God to help me to be quick to listen and understand, slow to talk or respond, and not so easily angered. Sometimes, I ask God to help me with it on multiple occasions throughout the day. I ask Him, as well, to help me with my attitude ("You must have the same attitude that Christ Jesus had." Philippians 2:5 NLT). I often pray and ask God for help in these areas, knowing how my flesh wants to do the contrary ("For the flesh lusts against the Spirit, and the Spirit against the flesh; and these are contrary to one another, so that you do not do the things that you wish." Galatians 5:17 NKJV) and realizing that I can slip at any moment, even in areas I'm currently standing strong in ("If you think you are standing strong, be careful not to fall." 1 Corinthians 10:12 NLT). Whether you're struggling to get out of something, need help breaking a bad habit, or just don't want fall in a certain area, you can always seek God's help. His Holy Spirit is available to guide and remind you of when you're about to mess up or sin.

Twenty-three

For even when we were with you, we commanded you this: If anyone will not work, neither shall he eat. For we hear that there are some who walk among you in a disorderly manner, not working at all, but are busybodies.

II Thessalonians 3:10-11 NKJV

If you're an able-bodied believer, you should be doing some type of work. And whatever occupation or career you chose to pursue, you should be engaging in kingdom building work, as a representative of Christ ("Now then, we are ambassadors for Christ, as though God were pleading through us: we implore you on Christ's behalf, be reconciled to God." II Corinthians 5:20 NKJV) Work helps you build things and contribute to the community and, possibly the world. Work generates financial resources. Through the avenue of work, significant and great relationships can be formed. The workplace can prompt you to pray fervently and seek God like never before. Work can help you focus less on yourself and more on others. Work can help you find, or give, you purpose. With the technology in place today, you can effectively work from anywhere in the world and be productive. When we're not working and we have a bunch idle time that isn't focused on bettering ourselves or others, it's way too easy and tempting to start meddling in others' affairs, causing disruption and preventing people who actually want to work, from getting their jobs done. Even if that isn't our intent.

Twenty-four

And whatever you do, do it heartily, as to the Lord and not to men, knowing that from the Lord you will receive the reward of the inheritance; for you serve the Lord Christ.

Colossians 3:23-24 NKJV

We should do things willingly, giving them our best efforts, while glorifying God, from whom our lasting rewards come. If you're going to spend your time doing something, whether you have your own business, work for an employee, house sit, change diapers, do lawncare, pick up trash, perform surgery, give consultations, serve in the military, play professional sports, coach, partner with a group, volunteer, or help someone with their homework, you should do it out of love (read 1 Corinthians 16:14) and enthusiastically, as opposed to begrudgingly or in a languid manner.

Twenty-five

Cast thy burden upon the Lord, and he shall sustain thee: he shall never suffer the righteous to be moved.

Psalms 55:22 KJV

You learn a lot when it's time to move. Whether it's packing up a two-bedroom apartment, three-bedroom condo or family household with a shed in the back. You'll come across things that haven't been used in so long, that you probably forgot about them. Clothes you haven't worn in years, papers you had in drawers, outdated gadgets, or toys that haven't been played with in over a decade. In the midst of all that packing, you realize you've been holding on to some useless stuff, that should have actually been given away, or disposed of months ago. Things that will NOT make the packing cut. Why? Because they haven't been and won't be a benefit or of use to you moving forward. Things that just aren't worth the time and effort to carry with you any further. They are outdated, serve no purpose, and take up space for more important things. The same applies to any burdens we've been carrying for years. Sometimes we don't even realize we still have them. It's important to cast them ALL on the Lord. Don't take them with you into the next day or season of your life. Do an inventory (it will require an honest self-examination and perhaps help from those closest to you) to find any hidden or open burdens in the way of you moving forward peacefully.

Twenty-six

So when he had received food, he was strengthened. Then Saul spent some days with the disciples at Damascus. Immediately he preached the Christ in the synagogues, that He is the Son of God. Then all who heard were amazed, and said, "Is this not he who destroyed those who called on this name in Jerusalem, and has come here for that purpose, so that he might bring them bound to the chief priests?" But Saul increased all the more in strength, and confounded the Jews who dwelt in Damascus, proving that this Jesus is the Christ.

Acts 9:19-22 NKJV

When Saul's doubters and critics were second guessing what he was doing for the Lord, He didn't argue, debate or plead his case; he just kept sharing and living the Word of God. If God has changed your life and you're continuously maturing, there will always be naysayers. But you don't have to go back and forth with them, in hopes of convincing them of the legitimacy of your change; just keep sharing and living out the word of God.

Twenty-seven

"Why does this Man speak blasphemies like this? Who can forgive sins but God alone?" But immediately, when Jesus perceived in His spirit that they reasoned thus within themselves, He said to them, "Why do you reason about these things in your hearts? Which is easier, to say to the paralytic, 'Your sins are forgiven you,' or to say, 'Arise, take up your bed and walk'? But that you may know that the Son of Man has power on earth to forgive sins" —He said to the paralytic, "I say to you, arise, take up your bed, and go to your house." Immediately he arose, took up the bed, and went out in the presence of them all, so that all were amazed and glorified God, saying, "We never saw anything like this!"

Mark 2:7-12 NKJV

Worldly hate can be favorable for a believer. When people doubt God or the abilities that He's given you, don't take it personally. Look at it as an opportunity for God to show out and get the glory. The very people hating on you could be the catalyst to God doing great works or even a miracle in your life.

Twenty-eight

And Sarai said unto Abram, Behold now, the Lord hath restrained me from bearing: I pray thee, go in unto my maid; it may be that I may obtain children by her. And Abram hearkened to the voice of Sarai. And Sarai Abram's wife took Hagar her maid the Egyptian, after Abram had dwelt ten years in the land of Canaan, and gave her to her husband Abram to be his wife. And he went in unto Hagar, and she conceived: and when she saw that she had conceived, her mistress was despised in her eyes.

Genesis 16:2-4 KJV

God could've closed up Hagar's womb and only permitted Sarai to get pregnant, birthing the heir to Abram, as He intended. But as we see here, there are times when God shows us the errors of our ways by letting the results of them become fully conceived (*Then when lust hath conceived, it bringeth forth sin: and sin, when it*

is finished, bringeth forth death. James 1:15
KJV). The result of that initial sin led to nations
(the descendants of Ishmael and Isaac) being at
war, even until this day. An ongoing feud that
has ruined some and taken the lives of many
others. Sarai and Abram had no clue that their
choice would lead to the amount of misery and
turmoil that it ultimately did. We can do what
we want outside of God's will, but we won't get
to decide the lasting effects or repercussions of
our disobedience.

Twenty-nine

So she turned to Abraham and demanded, "Get rid of that slave woman and her son. He is not going to share the inheritance with my son, Isaac. I won't have it!"

Genesis 21:10 NLT

Oh, NOW you don't want him to be the heir or have any parts of the inheritance. But wasn't that actually Sarai's initial plan? For the son that her husband had with her handmaiden/servant (she called her that when she suggested it but now, she's referred to as a slave) to be the heir? Isn't it funny how when we make our own plans and they clash with what God had ordained for us (Sarah had given birth to Isaac at this point) that we end up despising and regretting the things that resulted from our rushed and ridiculous plans? Trust in God's plans and His perfect timing.

Thirty

O Lord, you have examined my heart and know everything about me. You know when I sit down or stand up. You know my thoughts even when I'm far away. You see me when I travel and when I rest at home. You know everything I do. You know what I am going to say even before I say it, Lord. You go before me and follow me. You place your hand of blessing on my head. Such knowledge is too wonderful for me, too great for me to understand! I can never escape from your Spirit! I can never get away from your presence! If I go up to heaven, you are there; if I go down to the grave, you are there. If I ride the wings of the morning, if I dwell by the farthest oceans, even there your hand will guide me, and your strength will support me. I could ask the darkness to hide me and the light around me to become night— but even in darkness I cannot hide from you. To you the night shines as bright

as day. Darkness and light are the same to you.
Psalms 139:1-12 NLT

If you can ever get to a place of complete honesty with God, it will liberate your soul and elate your spirit. Not only can't you hide from God, but your thoughts can't be masked either. So why try to be disingenuous or disguise your feelings? Since God loves you in spite of your thoughts (He already knew you'd think them and He still sent His only begotten Son to die in your place, before you could even formulate your first sinful thought,) why not be transparent with Him? He already knows everything about your past, present and future. Save yourself the time and trouble of playing games with God and build a healthy relationship with Him instead.

Thirty-one

You made all the delicate, inner parts of my body and knit me together in my mother's womb. Thank you for making me so wonderfully complex! Your workmanship is marvelous—how well I know it. You watched me as I was being formed in utter seclusion, as I was woven together in the dark of the womb. You saw me before I was born. Every day of my life was recorded in your book. Every moment was laid out before a single day had passed. How precious are your thoughts about me, O God. They cannot be numbered! I can't even count them; they outnumber the grains of sand! And when I wake up, you are still with me!

Psalms 139:13-18 NLT

You didn't just come off some random rudimentary assembly line, nor did God have someone else orchestrate or oversee your conception. You were designed perfectly by a perfect God who makes no mistakes. Every day of your life was mapped out and seen through by an omniscient God, before you took your first breath. You are a blessing and far from an accident. Your parents might have planned to have you but God alone grants successful life. Someone interested in you may struggle to name ten valid reasons why they're so called "in love" with you, but God's fondness for you can't be counted. He watches over and protects you while you sleep and is right there when you awaken from your slumber. Thank God for being who He is!!! I would've used an adjective to describe Him, but there aren't any words in the human language to properly depict His unrivaled attributes.

Thirty-two

Commit thy works unto the Lord, and thy thoughts shall be established.

Proverbs 16:3 KJV

If you commit the things you do to God, He has a way of strategically guiding your thoughts on those matters. Once your thoughts are firmly established -not wavering- then your actions won't be all over the place, which will lead to stable success.

Thirty-three

Draw near to God and He will draw near to you. Cleanse your hands, you sinners; and purify your hearts, you double-minded.

James 4:8 NKJV

I love how technology enhances the things we do and enjoy in life. It makes the things we utilize, easier and convenient. One thing that I take advantage of daily, is Bluetooth capability. I connect my phone to a portable speaker, which allows me to hear my favorite songs and listen to several podcasts. As good as the range of that speaker is, sometimes I move too far away from it, and the sound becomes distorted or goes completely out. The same can be said when we drift from God due to laziness, failure to properly prioritize, neglect, or just down right purposely ignoring and quenching His Holy Spirit. But when we draw near to Him, the connection becomes stronger and stronger, allowing us to distinctly hear His message. Consistent time spent with God will help diminish any perceived confusion on your part. God's word is clear, His direction righteous, and His path straight. If you're having trouble making out or understanding what He's saying to you or where He's leading you, try moving closer to Him while He moves closer to you. I guarantee the "signal" will become undeniable.

Thirty-four

Now the word of the LORD came to Jonah the son of Amittai, saying, "Arise, go to Nineveh, that great city, and cry out against it; for their wickedness has come up before Me." But Jonah arose to flee to Tarshish from the presence of the LORD. He went down to Joppa, and found a ship going to Tarshish; so he paid the fare, and went down into it, to go with them to Tarshish from the presence of the LORD. But the LORD sent out a great wind on the sea, and there was a mighty tempest on the sea, so that the ship was about to be broken up.

Jonah 1:1-4 NKJV

I'm going to let you in on a secret, that you don't have to thank or pay me for. If you plan on going against what you know God has told you to do, you'll end up wasting time, energy and money. I'll throw this one in for free as well: If you're a child of God and you've made up your mind to flee from the way He's leading you, turn back as SOON as possible. If not, you'll inevitably run into a big enough storm that will have you all broken up and "force" you to go back the route He initially designed for you to follow.

Thirty-five

Then the mariners were afraid; and every man cried out to his god, and threw the cargo that was in the ship into the sea, to lighten the load. But Jonah had gone down into the lowest parts of the ship, had lain down, and was fast asleep. So the captain came to him, and said to him, "What do you mean, sleeper? Arise, call on your God; perhaps your God will consider us, so that we may not perish."

Jonah 1:5-6 NKJV

You can choose to ignore the consequences of your disobedience or even act as if it doesn't really bother you. But, regardless of how you deal with it, it usually affects those that are close to or around you in one way or another. Refusing to connect the dots of your sin to the objurgated aftermath, won't stop others from recognizing it. Have you decided, like Jonah, to just sleep and hope things will get better without you submitting to God or doing what He's called you to do? If so, be prepared for the predictable wake up call to come. God will only let you snooze for so long, before you have to face reality.

Thirty-six

"Throw me into the sea," Jonah said, "and it will become calm again. I know that this terrible storm is all my fault." Instead, the sailors rowed even harder to get the ship to the land. But the stormy sea was too violent for them, and they couldn't make it.

Jonah 1:12-13 NLT

They asked the man of God for the solution but when he gave it, they did their own thing instead. Are you like that as well? Do you seek godly advice, get it, and still do what you feel is best; only making things harder on yourself?

Then the sailors picked Jonah up and threw him into the raging sea, and the storm stopped at once! The sailors were awestruck by the Lord's great power, and they offered him a sacrifice and vowed to serve him.
Jonah 1:15-16 NLT

Thirty-seven

Now when He got into a boat, His disciples followed Him. And suddenly a great tempest arose on the sea, so that the boat was covered with the waves. But He was asleep. Then His disciples came to Him and awoke Him, saying, "Lord, save us! We are perishing!" But He said to them, "Why are you fearful, O you of little faith?" Then He arose and rebuked the winds and the sea, and there was a great calm.

Matthew 8:23-26 NKJV

God doesn't want us living a life full of fear and trepidation (*For God hath not given us the spirit of fear; but of power, and of love, and of a sound mind.* 2 Timothy 1:7 KJV). Jesus is in control of every situation, no matter how dreadful or intimidating it may appear. Practice putting your trust and faith in Him. Then when new storms arise (if you keep living, they most certainly will), remember the past storms, trials and situations that He's saved you from. That should help reassure you, while putting your sudden fears at ease. As you continue to mature in your faith, I pray that you have peace in any and every storm. Even if it doesn't make sense to be so calm and serene to the outside world. *And the peace of God, which passeth all understanding, shall keep your hearts and minds through Christ Jesus.* Philippians 4:7 KJV

Thirty-eight

But the men marvelled, saying, What manner of man is this, that even the winds and the sea obey him!

Matthew 8:27 KJV

Sometimes we can get so caught up in the physical and what we see, that we easily miss the spiritual aspect (God) in it all. For example, in the book of Mark, Jesus is trying to teach His disciples some spiritual principles but they're too busy thinking about the physical to understand, *And he charged them, saying, Take heed, beware of the leaven of the Pharisees, and of the leaven of Herod. And they reasoned among themselves, saying, It is because we have no bread. And when Jesus knew it, he saith unto them, Why reason ye, because ye have no bread? perceive ye not yet, neither understand? have ye your heart yet hardened? Having eyes, see ye not? and having ears, hear ye not? and do ye not remember? When I brake the five loaves among five thousand, how many baskets full of fragments took ye up? They say unto him, Twelve. And when the seven among four thousand, how many baskets full of fragments took ye up? And they said, Seven. And he said unto them, How is it that ye do not understand?* Mark 8:15-21 KJV

Focusing on material things, personal deadlines on the job, someone you like, or even food, can cloud your spiritual mind. Instead, make God and His Word the focal point of all that you do, and the rest will work out; glory to God. *Therefore take no thought, saying, What shall we eat? or, What shall we drink? or, Wherewithal shall we be clothed? (For after all these things do the Gentiles seek:) for your heavenly Father knoweth that ye have need of all these things. But seek ye first the kingdom of God, and his righteousness; and all these things shall be added unto you.* Matthew 6:31-33 KJV

Thirty-nine

But forget all that— it is nothing compared to what I am going to do. For I am about to do something new. See, I have already begun! Do you not see it? I will make a pathway through the wilderness. I will create rivers in the dry wasteland. The wild animals in the fields will thank me, the jackals and owls, too, for giving them water in the desert. Yes, I will make rivers in the dry wasteland so my chosen people can be refreshed.

Isaiah 43:18-20 NLT

It can be extremely difficult to let go of old things, habits, environments or mindsets. But the new things that God wants to establish in your life will not only enhance yours but exceedingly bless others as well. Even the wild animals would give thanks for the new and refreshing things, God did in the life of His chosen ones. Similarly, others will praise and thank God for the abundance of blessings that He showers you with, as they benefit from the residue of His favor on and in your life.

Forty

For the kingdom of heaven is like a man traveling to a far country, who called his own servants and delivered his goods to them.

Matthew 25:14 NKJV

This passage, commonly referred to as "The Parable of the Talents," is a familiar one, if you've heard at least a year's worth of sermons. It wasn't until recently, that I realized the men were his own servants. Not just some random strangers in the city that he selected. There was a relationship there. He knew them well. Therefore, he knew who had the capacity to handle what. If you read the entire parable, you'll notice that two of them kept the main thing the main thing, when asked to give an account. The third one immediately laid out his reasoning for his lack of effort.

Another thing I perceived, is that it wasn't even about the money he left with them to manage; it was about them being good stewards over what they were entrusted with. The 28th verse confirms that it wasn't about money (him wanting them to make more, just so he could take and use it), because he gave the talent of the lazy servant to the one who had doubled his original five. Although there was a relationship between the Lord and his servants, the third one didn't know him as wise. If he had, he would've known that his Lord would've never assigned him a task that he was ill equipped or unable to accomplish. The excuse-making servant was gifted but he didn't use his gifts, resulting in him being unprofitable and not useful for the Lord's kingdom. That led to him being cast out of his lord's presence; no longer receiving grace, causing a myriad of agonizing issues to ensue. *Now throw this useless servant into outer darkness, where there will be weeping and gnashing of teeth.*
Matthew 25:30 NLT

Forty-one

Give, and it shall be given unto you; good measure, pressed down, and shaken together, and running over, shall men give into your bosom. For with the same measure that ye mete withal it shall be measured to you again.

Luke 6:38 KJV

Could fear of not having, influence you to not give to God? I hope not, because this verse makes it clear that the amount you give is directly correlated to the amount you'll receive. I know this can be tough when you already don't have a lot, and what little you have seems to never be enough. Have you considered that it could be because you aren't sowing into God's kingdom? *Now therefore, thus says the LORD of hosts: "Consider your ways! "You have sown much, and bring in little; You eat, but do not have enough; You drink, but you are not filled with drink; You clothe yourselves, but no one is* warm; *And he who earns wages, Earns wages to put into a bag with holes.*" Haggai 1:5-6 NKJV We should be clinging to God's unchanging word (*I cling to Your testimonies; O LORD, do not put me to shame!* Psalms 119:31 NKJV) instead of possessions and money. In accordance with Philippians 4:19, God will supply all of our needs. Don't allow your unbelief in His promise to provide or your stinginess to keep you in a perpetual cycle of deficiency.

Forty-two

Ye ask, and receive not, because ye ask amiss, that ye may consume it upon your lusts.

James 4:3 KJV

If you took all the petitions out of your prayers, how long would they be? In other words, what percentage of your prayer life consist of thankfulness, adoration, praise and gratefulness as opposed to only asking God for things? What percentage of it, is concerned with the needs and welfare of others? What percentage of it lines up with God's will instead of your personal bucket list of pleasures?

Forty-three

But let patience have her perfect work, that ye may be perfect and entire, wanting nothing.

James 1:4 KJV

If you practice making yourself wait and denying your flesh, it won't be an issue when you have to hold off for someone or there's a delay in receiving something you want. When you're denied something you desire, it won't be the end of the world, because you've committed yourself to patience. Not to mention, God will RARELY be on your timetable, so it would behoove you to have patience, while waiting for the promises to occur.

For ye have need of patience, that, after ye have done the will of God, ye might receive the promise.

Hebrews 10:36 KJV

Forty-four

When pride cometh, then cometh shame: but with the lowly is wisdom.

Proverbs 11:2 KJV

If we're fortunate to keep living, we'll all be called on to lead in some capacity of form within our lifespan. Leaders must make a good deal of decisions. And since none of us are perfect, as a leader, you will make mistakes. Admitting when you're wrong is what separates common leaders from great ones. If you don't walk around, puffed up, as if you know everything, it will make it easier to accept the responsibility of any bad choices. If you're humble, it will aid in apologizing for your errors as well. And lastly, if you don't harshly criticize others, as if you're perfect, when they mess up, it won't be an immense deal when you fail. No one wants to work for or with a leader that takes all the credit and none of the blame. Don't let your pride stop you from accepting responsibility for your faults and ruin the workplace or your relationships.

A man's pride shall bring him low: but honour shall uphold the humble in spirit.

Proverbs 29:23 KJV

Forty-five

So he left Asaph and his brothers there before the ark of the covenant of the LORD to minister before the ark regularly, as every day's work required;

I Chronicles 16:37 NKJV

In this instance, the word minister is used as a verb. It means to serve, doing whatever is needed. Just like Asaph and his brothers were called to serve the Lord daily, so are we. There are no days off when you're living for the only true and living God. We should be worshiping and serving Him all the days of our lives. No matter how menial or valuable the task is in our eyes, we should perform it wholeheartedly. And whatever He calls us to do, He will empower us to complete it.

Forty-six

But he that is greatest among you shall be your servant.

Matthew 23:11 KJV

Worldly phrases like, "get all you can" don't apply in the kingdom of God. If anything, it would be, "Serve as much and as many as you possibly can." Your greatness isn't based on how much you can get out of others, but on how you give from your heart, while serving and providing for the needs of others. That includes reaching the lost for Christ and helping to build up believers. So, how great do you want to be? The choice is yours, and the only thing stopping you is you.

Forty-seven

David and all the people of Israel were celebrating before the Lord, singing songs and playing all kinds of musical instruments—lyres, harps, tambourines, castanets, and cymbals. But when they arrived at the threshing floor of Nacon, the oxen stumbled, and Uzzah reached out his hand and steadied the Ark of God. Then the Lord's anger was aroused against Uzzah, and God struck him dead because of this. So Uzzah died right there beside the Ark of God. David was angry because the Lord's anger had burst out against Uzzah. He named that place Perez-uzzah (which means "to burst out against Uzzah"), as it is still called today.

2 Samuel 6:5-8 NLT

In the fifth chapter of the second book of Samuel, David becomes the King of all Israel. He captures the stronghold of Zion (which then becomes known as The City of David) and then defeats the Philistines. Needless to say, he's on a roll and living the good life. His next step is to bring the ark of God from Judah up to Jerusalem. In verse five above, we see that everyone is celebrating and having a great time. That is, until Uzzah violates one of Gods' commandments, trying to do what he felt was a noble gesture, by stopping the ark from falling. Uzzah's death angered David. His anger developed into fear, which caused him to not bring the ark into the City of David. Has an incident or something transpired in your life that has made you angry at God? Have you forgotten your purpose? Have you lost your initial joy or disregarded all the victories He's carried you through in the past? Go to Him honestly about how you feel. Allow Him to comfort, edify and get you back on the right track.

Forty-eight

The Lord your God will drive those nations out ahead of you little by little. You will not clear them away all at once, otherwise the wild animals would multiply too quickly for you.

Deuteronomy 7:22 NLT

We're not even that smart to know what's best. I know we think we do, when we ask God for certain things, but the truth is we have no clue majority of the time. God knows the beginning from the end. Just like with the children of Israel. He was enough not to destroy all of their enemies at once. Had he done so, the wild animals would've multiplied and been a beast to contend with, pardon the pun. You may be petitioning God like, "Lord just get me through this trial and I'm GOOD," not knowing if He instantly wipes that problem away, another one would consume you just as fast, if not faster. Trust in the Lord's timing. He may be delaying your breakthrough or answer to your prayer for your best interest. Allow Him to work it all out (See Romans 8:28).

Forty-nine

It is honorable for a man to stop striving, since any fool can start a quarrel.

Proverbs 20:3 NKJV

You think you're doing something because you're arguing with strangers online, via your phone, getting likes? Stop it. Anyone can debate a profile picture. But an honorable and wise person will not escalate or waste time quarrelling online or in person. Don't let the trolls, hateful souls, or ignorant people, pull you into their foolish world of ongoing comments.

Fifty

A sound heart is life to the body, but envy is rottenness to the bones.

Proverbs 14:30 NKJV

Nowadays, you can compare yourself to millions of people that you will never meet nor never know their true struggles. Don't be fooled by the perfect life they display, filters they use, angles they shoot from, or computer-generated images they incorporate. All of that daily comparison can quickly lead to envy, covetousness, and sadness. Theodore Roosevelt said it best, "Comparison is the thief of joy."

Fifty-one

For if there should come into your assembly a man with gold rings, in fine apparel, and there should also come in a poor man in filthy clothes, and you pay attention to the one wearing the fine clothes and say to him, "You sit here in a good place," and say to the poor man, "You stand there," or, "Sit here at my footstool," have you not shown partiality among yourselves, and become judges with evil thoughts?

James 2:2-4 NKJV

Generally speaking, how you perceive someone is how you receive them. Whether it's based on what they drive, where they live, what university they graduated from, their job, how they smell, what attire they have on, how their hair looks, the color of their skin, how they're built, what sex they are, what their sexual orientation is, or the corner they're standing on. God forbids us from treating people special (showing favortism) or less than, (discrimination) just because we like how they look or what title they hold. Don't let your prejudiced attitudes influence or determine how you treat God's creation.

Fifty-two

A person without self-control is like a city with broken-down walls.

Proverbs 25:28 NLT

If a person doesn't put up barriers, establish boundaries, have standards, or guidelines to help channel their choices, they'll end up allowing and doing anything. Not only that, but in doing so, their value will be vastly diminished. That's why it's important to have the biblical morals and accompanying discipline to not violate them incessantly.

Fifty-three

*The king asked, "Well, how can I help you?"
With a prayer to the God of heaven, I replied, "If
it please the king, and if you are pleased with
me, your servant, send me to Judah to rebuild
the city where my ancestors are buried." The
king, with the queen sitting beside him, asked,
"How long will you be gone? When will you
return?" After I told him how long I would be
gone, the king agreed to my request. I also said
to the king, "If it please the king, let me have
letters addressed to the governors of the
province west of the Euphrates River, instructing
them to let me travel safely through their
territories on my way to Judah. And please give
me a letter addressed to Asaph, the manager of
the king's forest, instructing him to give me
timber. I will need it to make beams for the
gates of the Temple fortress, for the city walls,
and for a house for myself." And the king
granted these requests, because the gracious
hand of God was on me.* Nehemiah 2:4-8 NLT

I've made it a way of life, to seek God before I set out to accomplish, gain or achieve anything. I also make sure to do like Nehemiah, once I receive what I prayed for, and give God the glory and praise. Getting what I desired wouldn't be complete without letting it be known that Jesus, whose gracious hands were on me, was the reason for my success. Lest I start feeling myself once I'm well established and I forget who was responsible for it all (see Deuteronomy 8:10-18)

Fifty-four

Jesus said to the people who believed in him,

"You are truly my disciples if you remain faithful

to my teachings. And you will know the truth,

and the truth will set you free."

John 8:31-32 NLT

Jesus informed the people who believed in Him,

that if they were truly His disciples, they would

remain faithful to His teachings. In other words,

be obedient to what He told and revealed to

them. Becoming a believer in God is just the

first step. An essential one, but only the initial

step. Jesus isn't as concerned with people

believing who He is, as much as He's concerned

that people obediently following Him. His great

commandment wasn't "go and make believers

of Me..." It was to go and make disciples, teaching them to observe/follow all the things that He Himself commands.

And Jesus came and spoke to them, saying, "All authority has been given to Me in heaven and on earth. Go therefore and make disciples of all the nations, baptizing them in the name of the Father and of the Son and of the Holy Spirit, teaching them to observe all things that I have commanded you; and lo, I am with you always, even to the end of the age." Amen.

Matthew 28:18-20 NKJV

Jesus desires learned followers who are obedient. Do you fall in that category or are you "just" a believer?

Fifty-five

The hand of the diligent will rule, But the lazy man will be put to forced labor.

Proverbs 12:24 NKJV

Outside of nepotism or the "good ole boy" system, anyone who wants to have a position of authority cannot dare be lazy. Hard workers tend to become leaders, managers, presidents and more, as opposed to just hired help. Diligence allows you to position yourself to take advantage of more freedoms, opportunities, partnerships, offers, promotions, etc. If you're diligent, you won't be limited or forced to accept whatever you can get.

Fifty-six

Then they said to one another, "Look, this dreamer is coming! Come therefore, let us now kill him and cast him into some pit; and we shall say, 'Some wild beast has devoured him.' We shall see what will become of his dreams!"

Genesis 37:19-20 NKJV

Joseph shared a vision that God showed him in a dream with his family. Needless to say, it wasn't received well. His brothers already hated him because his father loved him more than all the brothers and let it be known. Although you should never dislike people, simply because another person likes them, or perhaps favors them more than you. But some of Joseph's brothers plotted to kill him one day. In doing so, they thought they would kill his dream. Perhaps they assumed it was just a dream that he had because he wanted that or constantly thought about it. Maybe they assumed he was merely bragging about what he hoped for. They didn't realize it was God's plan. And when God has a plan for you, NOBODY can foil it. He is fully aware of who will try to prevent and derail His plans, well before He activates them. Whenever people try to stop God's plan, they end up helping it succeed. Never be discouraged or fearful when people try to kill God's vision for your life, ministry, work, or family. God's plans are similar to when He sends His infallible word; they will not be void or incomplete.

Fifty-seven

*But without faith it is impossible to please him:
for he that cometh to God must believe that he
is, and that he is a rewarder of them that
diligently seek him.*

Hebrews 11:6 KJV

People will tirelessly search for something to
watch or stream. They'll also force themselves
to watch something they came across, even if
it's not really what they really wanted to see.
Many will watch old stuff, that they've
previously seen, more than once. Some of those
same people can be heard saying they don't
have time to read the Word of God, assemble
with fellow believers, or search the scriptures
diligently. I've also heard, "I already read that
before" as they disregard re-reading or listening
to a message they once heard. I guess they only
benefit from re-watching movies or shows?

Fifty-eight

I walked by the field of a lazy person, the vineyard of one with no common sense. I saw that it was overgrown with nettles. It was covered with weeds, and its walls were broken down. Then, as I looked and thought about it, I learned this lesson: A little extra sleep, a little more slumber, a little folding of the hands to rest— then poverty will pounce on you like a bandit; scarcity will attack you like an armed robber.

Proverbs 24:30-34 NLT

Here we see a lazy person who was blessed to have a fruitful field. Had he worked it or given some actual effort, he would've been able to continually reap the benefits. But instead, the very thing that God blessed him with, was going to waste, due to his laziness. We also see that a lesson was learned. It's a favorable thing to be able to learn lessons from other people's mistakes as opposed to having to learn from your own errors. That's referred to as, "finding out the hard way." Take heed to the Word of God, as well as, the inevitable consequences that befall those who ignore it.

Fifty-nine

Those who are dominated by the sinful nature think about sinful things, but those who are controlled by the Holy Spirit think about things that please the Spirit. So letting your sinful nature control your mind leads to death. But letting the Spirit control your mind leads to life and peace.

Romans 8:5-6 NLT

We can tell what we're dominated by and consumed with, by what we think about the most. That's why it's important to take an honest evaluation of your daily thought life. I can assure you, whatever you constantly think about, are the things you will attempt to do the most. That's why those sinful thoughts, as sure as they come, have to be brought into captivity, under the obedience of Christ. Because when fully grown and lived out, they lead to death. But when we consider and mediate on the things of God, we'll reap the fruits of joy, peace and prosperity.

Sixty

*Dear brothers and sisters, pattern your lives
after mine, and learn from those who follow our
example. For I have told you often before, and I
say it again with tears in my eyes, that there are
many whose conduct shows they are really
enemies of the cross of Christ. They are headed
for destruction. Their god is their appetite, they
brag about shameful things, and they think only
about this life here on earth.*

Philippians 3:17-19 NLT

Paul encouraged the believers living in Philippi
(a city in ancient eastern Macedonia) to pattern
their lives after his, and other followers, who
were patterning theirs after Christ. He told
them that they should learn from the believers
who were actually living what they'd learned
about Jesus. Those were the examples they
needed to follow. Because there were many,

whose lifestyles confirmed that they were really enemies of God, contrary to their profession of faith in Jesus Christ, as their Lord and Savior. The way they lived, and the frivolous things they bragged about, showed who their god was and where their daily focus was. If people patterned their lifestyles after yours, would they be headed for destruction, or the righteous way to life?

Sixty-one

Later the leaders sent some Pharisees and supporters of Herod to trap Jesus into saying something for which he could be arrested. "Teacher," they said, "we know how honest you are. You are impartial and don't play favorites. You teach the way of God truthfully. Now tell us—is it right to pay taxes to Caesar or not?"

Mark 12:13-14 NLT

Jesus (God in the flesh) never lied (reference Titus 1:2), nor did he show favoritism to anyone based on outward appearance, background, social or economic status (reference Acts 10:34). With authority, He shared and taught God's word freely. Likewise, when we share the word with others, it shouldn't be based on anything but the truth, and out of love. It should never be changed or twisted to appease anyone or fit the agenda of the day. People, popularity, opinions, laws, rules, and many other things are constantly changing. But God and His Word remain the same. People tried to confound Jesus with their "loaded" questions, so don't be dismayed if they try to trip you up from time to time, concerning His Word. If you're sharing and doing, what thus says the Lord, then you'll always be right regardless of any other popular opinions formed against you. When certain groups aligned and plotted against Jesus, He knew their hypocrisy, because God knows the heart of men. There's no fooling Him with trick questions to see if His word is true. Just like you can't fool Him by any request made with promises you won't keep. At one point, *Jesus replied, "Your mistake is that you don't know the Scriptures, and you don't know the power of God."* (Mark 12:24 NLT) Don't make the same mistake as they did.

Sixty-two

In the multitude of words sin is not lacking, but he who restrains his lips is wise.

Proverbs 10:19 NKJV

Honestly, we aren't knowledgeable enough to talk nonstop/24-7, without sinning. Usually the sin comes by us exaggerating, trying to impress others, magnifying ourselves, gossiping, wasting time, or spreading false information that we assumed to be true, without verifying it. Use wisdom and keep some stuff to yourself, while taking advantage of your eyes and ears to learn more than you currently know, or thought you knew.

A fool uttereth all his mind: but a wise man keepeth it in till afterwards.

Proverbs 29:11 KJV

Sixity-three

*Because God's children are human beings—
made of flesh and blood—the Son also became
flesh and blood. For only as a human being
could he die, and only by dying could he break
the power of the devil, who had the power of
death. Only in this way could he set free all who
have lived their lives as slaves to the fear of
dying.*

Hebrews 2:14-15 NLT

Jesus loves us SO MUCH, that He sacrificed His
comfort, extolment, privileges and life (to name
a few), took on the form of a mere human, and
endured a humiliating death on the cross, for
the sins of humanity. Jesus left a perfect place,
where He was properly adored, worshipped and
honored, to live in a dying, ungrateful, and
sinful earth, so we would have the opportunity
to be reconciled to God. Jesus paid a price we
could never pay, while snatching the victory and

sting that death was holding over our heads. He was the perfect sacrifice and understands completely whatever we go through (read Hebrews 4:14-16). He knows firsthand what it's like to be tired, misunderstood, hated, persecuted, lied on, misused, unappreciated, back stabbed, hurt, abandoned by friends, spit on, beat, discredited, alone and more. And through it all, He was humble and obedient, (Having the power to stop it but choosing the Father's will over His own feelings) even to the point of death.

Sixty-four

Riches do not profit in the day of wrath, but righteousness delivers from death.

Proverbs 11:4 NKJV

How valuable is money to the person whose plane is about to crash? What's cash going to do when you have an acutely debilitating and incurable disease? Can riches stop the wealthy from contracting HIV? Is money helpful, if you're being robbed and you, along with your family, is about to be killed for it? How much does it cost to bring a loved-one back to life? If riches can be nullified on earth when certain things go awry, how can you reasonably expect them to have any influence during judgment day? At the end of the day, living righteously has more value than all the gold on earth.

Sixty-five

People do not despise a thief If he steals to satisfy himself when he is starving. Yet when he is found, he must restore sevenfold; He may have to give up all the substance of his house.

Proverbs 6:30-31 NKJV

People can be understanding when someone commits a crime like theft, when they're only trying to feed themselves or their family. But even then, when found and charged, they have to pay the penalty. Likewise, God is very understanding. He knows your motive and mindset when you say stuff like, "God knows my heart." I can assure you that He DOES know your heart and that if you sin, instead of trusting Him to provide or to do things His way, you'll still reap the consequences of those sins in due season. And it may be more than what you signed up for.

Sixty-six

*Now we are being punished because of our
wickedness and our great guilt. But we have
actually been punished far less than we deserve,
for you, our God, have allowed some of us to
survive as a remnant.*

Ezra 9:13 NLT

Ezra was aware of the GREATNESS of God's
mercy. He recognized that God does not give us
all that we deserve for our wrong doings or
issue the type of punishment that we would on
others, if they kept hurting us. Especially if we
had the power to do so. In verses 6 and 7 he
details their numerous sins and constant
transgressions. *I prayed, "O my God, I am utterly
ashamed; I blush to lift up my face to you. For
our sins are piled higher than our heads, and our
guilt has reached to the heavens. From the days
of our ancestors until now, we have been
steeped in sin. That is why we and our kings and*

our priests have been at the mercy of the pagan
kings of the land. We have been killed, captured,
robbed, and disgraced, just as we are today."
Ezra 9:6-7 NLT

Yes, there were some grave consequences for
their sins, just as there are in our own lives. But
God does not completely wipe us out, give up
on us, or forsake us. He's long suffering and
loves us in an incomprehensible way.

Regardless of the severity of His reprimand and
discipline, His ultimate goal is to reconcile us to
Himself. Thank God that He cares enough about
you to correct you when needed, while being
utterly merciful.

Sixty-seven

For you were bought at a price; therefore glorify God in your body and in your spirit, which are God's.

I Corinthians 6:20 NKJV

I've never been one to give unsolicited relationship advice, but I will share something with you that may ease the blow of heartbreak or prevent you from being crushed by disappointment. Are you ready for it? You don't own ANYONE. God bought them with a price, not you. And although you may be willing to die for them, you still won't own them, neither will you have paid the price that could free them from the power of sin. If you keep that in mind, along with the fact that people are their own person, make their own choices, and reap the consequences of their own mistakes, then it can help you if they do talk to or engage in something with another person. I know some people who will lose their cool, if who they're with or want to be with, even likes another person's pictures. No matter how nice you are, how helpful you've been, or how much you've provided and cared for them, you don't own them. This applies to your children, fiancé, spouse, crush, date, or soulmate. You don't even own the possessions you have. They ALL belong to God and you can't take any of them with you in the afterlife or claim them there (reference Matthew 22:30.) If you have been, you can stop saying that you'll be with them forever, because you won't. This is not to discourage anyone who is madly "in love" but rather to give you a better perspective in your relationships. If anything, I pray that it helps you truly value and appreciate the time you have with them on earth, since it won't last forever. And of course, to remind you, to always keep God first, never putting anyone or anything above your relationship with Him.

Sixty-eight

Now Peter and John went up together to the temple at the hour of prayer, the ninth hour. And a certain man lame from his mother's womb was carried, whom they laid daily at the gate of the temple which is called Beautiful, to ask alms from those who entered the temple; who, seeing Peter and John about to go into the temple, asked for alms. And fixing his eyes on him, with John, Peter said, "Look at us." So he gave them his attention, expecting to receive something from them. Then Peter said, "Silver and gold I do not have, but what I do have I give you: In the name of Jesus Christ of Nazareth, rise up and walk." And he took him by the right hand and lifted him up, and immediately his feet and ankle bones received strength. So he, leaping up, stood and walked and entered the temple with them—walking, leaping, and praising God. And all the people saw him walking and praising God.

Acts 3:1-8 NKJV

Peter and John saw a person in need and shared what they had. Turns out what they had, was far more than what the man in need had even asked for. Kind of like when we ask God for something and put our hope in Him, He's able to exceed that expectation and do far more than we actually thought. We may ask for some money to meet a need or want, but God blesses us way beyond that to where we even forget about the little money we initially asked for. The word of God has life-changing power. Power that transcends your typical or situational desires. Do you have God's Word in you? Are you able to share it when someone's in need? You can't share what you don't have. We should be continually seeking God's Word for ourselves, so when the opportunity comes, and it always does, we'll be able to share what we have and meet the needs of others. Glory to God.

Sixty-nine

So he went to Zarephath. As he arrived at the gates of the village, he saw a widow gathering sticks, and he asked her, "Would you please bring me a little water in a cup?" As she was going to get it, he called to her, "Bring me a bite of bread, too." But she said, "I swear by the Lord your God that I don't have a single piece of bread in the house. And I have only a handful of flour left in the jar and a little cooking oil in the bottom of the jug. I was just gathering a few sticks to cook this last meal, and then my son and I will die." But Elijah said to her, "Don't be afraid! Go ahead and do just what you've said, but make a little bread for me first. Then use what's left to prepare a meal for yourself and your son. For this is what the Lord, the God of Israel, says: There will always be flour and olive oil left in your containers until the time when the Lord sends rain and the crops grow again!" So she did as Elijah said, and she and Elijah and her family continued to eat for many days.

There was always enough flour and olive oil left in the containers, just as the Lord had promised through Elijah.

1 Kings 17:10-16 NLT

When Elijah told the widow to make him some bread first, she could've become frustrated, gotten an attitude, and replied, "I don't have a lot and you want what little I do have? Didn't I tell you that this is ALL we have and we're about to die?" Not giving has the potential to kill you slowly (that's what would have happened, if she had said no and continued with her initial plan), while giving can open up the windows of heaven, allowing God to pour out blessings on you for years to come, making sure you always have enough.

Seventy

The LORD by wisdom founded the earth; By understanding He established the heavens; By His knowledge the depths were broken up, And clouds drop down the dew.

Proverbs 3:19-20 NKJV

In case you read that too fast, read it again but slowly and with purpose, visualizing what occurred. Did you notice the amazingly splendid things, that God was able to accomplish by using wisdom, understanding, and knowledge? When He instructs us to get wisdom, knowledge and understanding, it's in part, to equip us to do, accomplish and create glorious things. Along with living a righteous life, of course.

The fear of the Lord is the beginning of wisdom: and the knowledge of the holy is understanding.

Proverbs 9:10 KJV

Grace and peace be multiplied unto you through the knowledge of God, and of Jesus our Lord, According as his divine power hath given unto us all things that pertain unto life and godliness, through the knowledge of him that hath called us to glory and virtue:
And beside this, giving all diligence, add to your faith virtue; and to virtue knowledge;

2 Peter 1:2-3, 5 KJV

Get wisdom! Get understanding! Do not forget, nor turn away from the words of my mouth. Wisdom is the principal thing; Therefore get wisdom. And in all your getting, get understanding. Exalt her, and she will promote you; She will bring you honor, when you embrace her.

Proverbs 4:5, 7-8 NKJV

Seventy-one

And Isaac spake unto Abraham his father, and said, My father: and he said, Here am I, my son. And he said, Behold the fire and the wood: but where is the lamb for a burnt offering?

And Abraham lifted up his eyes, and looked, and behold behind him a ram caught in a thicket by his horns: and Abraham went and took the ram, and offered him up for a burnt offering in the stead of his son. And Abraham called the name of that place Jehovah–jireh: as it is said to this day, In the mount of the Lord it shall be seen.

Genesis 22:7, 13-14 KJV

You don't have to know how, as long as you know God. Isaac saw the wood, him and his father. But He didn't see the lamb. In verse 8, Abraham told his son that the Lord would provide. What do you tell yourself, family or friends when no one sees how it's going to work? When they're unsure of where the money, help or healing will come from? How God provides, often times is mind-boggling. I stopped trying to figure it out a long time ago and just trusted that He would. The only thing that my trying to "guess" the way did, was occupy my thoughts and at times, led to my trying to force the way I wrongly assumed it would happen. Don't rush or worry; in God's perfect timing, His divine providence will be seen.

Seventy-two

And looking at Jesus as He walked, he said, "Behold the Lamb of God!" The two disciples heard him speak, and they followed Jesus.

John 1:36-37 NKJV

As ambassadors of Christ, we must point out the Lamb of God to others and pray that they will listen to His word, accept His gift of salvation, and follow Him.

Seventy-three

"Our fathers worshiped on this mountain, and you Jews say that in Jerusalem is the place where one ought to worship." Jesus said to her, "Woman, believe Me, the hour is coming when you will neither on this mountain, nor in Jerusalem, worship the Father. You worship what you do not know; we know what we worship, for salvation is of the Jews. But the hour is coming, and now is, when the true worshipers will worship the Father in spirit and truth; for the Father is seeking such to worship Him. God is Spirit, and those who worship Him must worship in spirit and truth."

John 4:20-24 NKJV

Thank God we don't have to travel to Mount Gerizim or the Temple in Jerusalem to worship Him. It's not where you go to worship the Lord, but the condition of your heart, that He's concerned with, when you do. Likewise, the methods and avenues we use to reach the lost for Christ has changed, and must continually evolve in order to reach an ever-changing world. The methods can be adjusted as long as the Message about Jesus stays true and untainted.

Seventy-four

"I have compassion on the multitude, because they have now continued with Me three days and have nothing to eat. And if I send them away hungry to their own houses, they will faint on the way; for some of them have come from afar."
So they ate and were filled, and they took up seven large baskets of leftover fragments.

Mark 8:2-3, 8 NKJV

Jesus had compassion on all that had been with Him for three days. They were following and listening to His word, fulfilling their spiritual needs, and He didn't want to send them away, lacking physically. That's the kind of awesome, loving, and concerned God we serve. If you're focused on Him and His word, He'll take care of you completely: spiritually and physically. He'll never send you away empty or worse off than when you came. Verse 8 in the NLT says, "They ate as much as they wanted. Afterward, the disciples picked up seven large baskets of leftover food."

They were able to get as much as they desired and still have plenty left over for anyone else who may have come along in need. Do you have any needs? Seek Jesus and continue to follow Him; He will provide an abundance.

Seventy-five

The very next day they began to eat unleavened bread and roasted grain harvested from the land. No manna appeared on the day they first ate from the crops of the land, and it was never seen again. So from that time on the Israelites ate from the crops of Canaan.

Joshua 5:11-12 NLT

Just to catch you up on things, at this point, the children of Israel have just crossed the Jordan River, the river God dried up, so they could cross over with ease. It was similar to what occurred when they strolled across the Red Sea, having left Egypt with the Egyptians' wealth. Joshua then circumcises the entire male population. He did that, because all the males who were old enough to fight when the Lord delivered them from Egypt had died in the wilderness. They celebrated the Passover, and the very next day they ate from the land. The manna God used to feed them for forty years (as He humbled them in the wilderness, testing them, to see what was in their hearts and whether they would keep His commandments) stopped appearing and was never seen again. God would now provide for them in different ways. The ways and resources may vary, and change suddenly, but the Way maker and Source will never change. Therefore, whether it's a ram in a bush, food delivery from ravens, manna from heaven, or any other way you can imagine, just know that God will always provide.

Seventy-six

*Now when he had left **speaking**, he said unto Simon, Launch out into the deep, and let down your nets for a draught. And Simon answering said unto him, Master, we have toiled all the night, and have taken nothing: nevertheless at thy word I will let down the net.*

Luke 5:4-5 KJV

Jesus was on Simon's boat, teaching the people on the shore. There's no way that Simon, being in the same boat, wouldn't have **heard** the word of the Lord. Afterwards, He gave Simon a personal word, specifically for his life. The "general" message that Simon heard Jesus share with the people, was able to increase his faith to the point, that when Jesus spoke to Him personally, he did what He was told, even when it didn't make sense. Pastor Doyle R. Adams is

known to say, "Faith doesn't make sense, it just works." Do you want to increase your faith?
So then faith cometh by hearing, and hearing by the word of God.

Romans 10:17 KJV

Seventy-seven

Then saith he unto his disciples, The harvest truly is plenteous, but the labourers are few;

Matthew 9:37 KJV

Way before the Covid-19 pandemic, Christ disciples were essential workers. There are plenty of people in need but a minimal number of trained workers, who are willing to sacrifice their time, effort, and sometimes safety to do the work of the Lord. Are you being trained weekly (in the medical field, it's known as continual education, aka CE's) to be an effective front-line worker in the Kingdom of God? Be honest, who wants an inexperienced worker that means well, handling life and death matters? We all would prefer a properly trained veteran instead of an undisciplined novice.

Seventy-eight

The lazy man does not roast what he took in hunting, But diligence is man's precious possession.

Proverbs 12:27 NKJV

It'd be unfeasible for someone to hunt but never cook what they gained, do their homework but not turn it in, or get a check and never cash it. Laziness prevents people from completing important things, like procrastination hinders them from starting. Diligence, however, is something precious that no one can steal from you. Diligence is the backbone of success and the battery that keeps overcomers going.

Seventy-nine

And when He had come out of the boat,
immediately there met Him out of the tombs a
man with an unclean spirit, who had his
dwelling among the tombs; and no one could
bind him, not even with chains,

Mark 5:2-3 NKJV

Isn't it intriguing how no one was trying to help
or find out how the man could get free from
what was tormenting him? Not only were they
unwilling to help, but they were also actually
trying to further bond him, "and no one could
bind him, not even with chains." As believers,
we should be trying to help people who struggle
with addictions, battle breaking bad habits, or
have strongholds, instead of ridiculing and
holding them down. The least we can do is point
them in the right direction, since true freedom
comes from God the Father, through the Son of

God. *Therefore if the Son makes you free, you shall be free indeed.* John 8:36 NKJV

Eighty

Then they scoffed, "He's just a carpenter, the son of Mary and the brother of James, Joseph, Judas, and Simon. And his sisters live right here among us." They were deeply offended and refused to believe in him. Then Jesus told them, "A prophet is honored everywhere except in his own hometown and among his relatives and his own family."

Mark 6:3-4 NLT

At times it may be a challenge, when you're trying to reach people you grew up around or family members and friends who think they "really" know you. When Jesus taught the word and did mighty works (see verses 1-2) in his own country, it actually offended some people. They couldn't see beyond the physical person they'd known growing up, in order to receive the word of God. Likewise, it could be difficult for people to get over your past or see the anointing that

God has on your life, which might hamper them from receiving the word you're trying to share. Everyone won't understand or welcome the gifts God has given you. They may even be offended by the great things He's doing through you. Don't get discouraged or let that stop you from being a blessing, encouraging others, and sharing the word of God wherever you go. Clearly, it didn't stop Jesus.

Eighty-one

*Then the Lord said to Joshua, "Do not be afraid
or discouraged. Take all your fighting men and
attack Ai, for I have given you the king of Ai, his
people, his town, and his land. You will destroy
them as you destroyed Jericho and its king. But
this time you may keep the plunder and the
livestock for yourselves. Set an ambush behind
the town."*

Joshua 8:1-2 NLT

Previously God had instructed the children of
Israel to not take any of the silver, gold, bronze
or iron from the plunder. That went against the
culture and worldly way of the time, because to
the victor, went the spoils.

*"Do not take any of the things set apart for
destruction, or you yourselves will be completely
destroyed, and you will bring trouble on the
camp of Israel. Everything made from silver,*

*gold, bronze, or iron is sacred to the Lord and
must be brought into his treasury."*
Joshua 6:18-19 NLT

I'd be foolish to try telling you exactly why God
instructed them not to take any of the spoils.
Plus, He's known to give a word that has a
multiplicity of meanings and benefits, in order
to test, mature and bless us. So, I won't give you
a list of reasons. However, I do know, without a
shadow of a doubt, that if you're obedient like
all of them except Achan was (read the 7th
chapter of Joshua) as well as patient, you'll
eventually reap a surplus that far outweighs
whatever you passed up.

*And let us not be weary in well doing: for in due
season we shall reap, if we faint not.*

Galatians 6:9 KJV

Eighty-two

Set your mind on things above, not on things on the earth.

Colossians 3:2 NKJV

Starting around middle school and continuing throughout college, students loved asking, "When am I ever going to use this?" if instructed to learn or test on something that didn't come naturally easy. Basically, if it didn't have a value to them beyond that class, they did NOT want to learn or pay attention to it. We should ask ourselves a similar question when thinking about, doing, or saying something: "Eternally speaking, will this be useful or valued beyond life on Earth?" If we can't unequivocally answer "Yes" then we shouldn't be focusing on it.

Eighty-three

A murderer's tormented conscience will drive him into the grave. Don't protect him!

Proverbs 28:17 NLT

I enjoy reenactment crime shows, whether it's unsolved mysteries, snapped, cold case files, or fatal attraction. Needless to say, the lion's share of murderers aren't the brightest crayons in the box. And the anomalies that aren't initially caught, due to their hairbrained mistakes, end up telling on themselves later. Their consciences eat at them until they have no rest or peace; then they share their flagitious secret, if not with the authorities, to someone else and that person rightly reports them. It's actually a relief to some of the murderers who get caught; the pressure of holding that monstrous crime in crumbles even the mentally strongest manslayers.

Eighty-four

My help comes from the LORD, who made heaven and earth! He will not let you stumble; the one who watches over you will not slumber. Indeed, he who watches over Israel never slumbers or sleeps.

Psalms 121:2-4 NLT

The same God who created the heavens and earth has made Himself available to us 24-7. We don't have to wait for a full moon, collect infinity stones, or make an unusual vow, to reach him. He literally doesn't get tired, weak, or ever need rejuvenating. You can get as much of Him as you want, when you want, and for as long as you want. If you're needing/wanting more of God, then that's on you because He's always there for His children and for any "stranger' searching for Him. The Creator, who's all-knowing, providing, protecting and powerful, is not only accessible, but actually WANTS to spend time with us. And that won't change. Psalms 121:7-8 NLT *The LORD keeps you from all harm and watches over your life. The LORD keeps watch over you as you come and go, both now and forever.*

Eighty-five

But as darkness fell and Jesus still hadn't come back, they got into the boat and headed across the lake toward Capernaum. Soon a gale swept down upon them, and the sea grew very rough. They had rowed three or four miles when suddenly they saw Jesus walking on the water toward the boat. They were terrified, but he called out to them, "Don't be afraid. I am here!" Then they were eager to let him in the boat, and immediately they arrived at their destination!

John 6:17-21 NLT

A gale is strong wind anywhere between 32-62 miles per hour. Jesus' disciples were caught in this situation without Him present. They were rowing and fighting against unfortunate circumstances and getting nowhere fast. I'm sure all of that fighting against the storm left them exhausted and frustrated. But when they welcomed Jesus aboard, it says they immediately arrived at their destination. As a matter of fact, the text says they were eager to let Him on board. We usually are after we've been swept up in something and realize we can't handle or manage it on our own. We'll all face strenuous situations in life, but if we allow Jesus on board and give control over to Him, we'll get to where we're going much faster and smoother. We weren't meant to struggle and fight on our own. We were meant to have our savior and master with us -Immanuel- leading the way. Don't leave God out of your thoughts or decisions. Unless of course, your goals are to squander as much time, money, and energy as humanly possible. Then by all means, leave Him out.

Eighty-six

*Death and life are in the power of the tongue,
and those who love it will eat its fruit.*

Proverbs 18:21 NKJV

Since death and life are in the power of the
tongue, I'm mindful of what I say and post. And
while I filter the toxic things that I think about
saying, I'm guilty of not speaking more things to
life. It's more than just not saying deadly words.
It's important that we're constantly speaking
life. A friend of mine said something the other
morning before he started his day. And sure
enough, what he spoke/claimed came to pass
that SAME night. It reminded me that I should
be doing the same, DAILY. Sometimes we need
to hear the truth in our hearts being proclaimed
out loud. Other times it's for those around us to
hear what we proclaim in Jesus' name, which
will allow them to give God the glory when they
see it happen. Your children and friends need to

hear it. It will strengthen and encourage them when they see God bless the fruit of your lips. Even your enemies need to hear it. Put them on notice and let them know the God you serve is in control and doing wonderful things in your life. Claim it. Don't be ashamed of speaking life and watching it unfold for all to see.

Eighty-seven

As the Scriptures say, "If you want to boast, boast only about the Lord." When people commend themselves, it doesn't count for much. The important thing is for the Lord to commend them.

2 Corinthians 10:17-18 NLT

If you're doing the work of the Lord, there's no reason to brag on yourself or magnify your talents. IF you're going to boast, bring attention to, or glorify anything, it should be God and God alone. Tooting your own horn is worthless. When God exalts and is well pleased with you, THEN it counts for something. Wouldn't it better to let God uplift and hold you up anyway? After all, His reach is much stronger and longer than yours.

Eighty-eight

I hate all your show and pretense— the hypocrisy of your religious festivals and solemn assemblies. I will not accept your burnt offerings and grain offerings. I won't even notice all your choice peace offerings. Away with your noisy hymns of praise! I will not listen to the music of your harps. Instead, I want to see a mighty flood of justice, an endless river of righteous living.

Amos 5:21-24 NLT

That's a profound and simply put statement, if I've ever seen one. God's isn't interested in your praise or offerings, if they aren't accompanied by a righteous lifestyle. In fact, He hates it. If you're defiantly disobedient and failing to show love and justice to all people, then the songs you sing, instruments you play, and prayers you pray, all sound like a bunch of useless noise to God, instead of beautiful uplifting sounds.

Eighty-nine

When they arrived back in Jerusalem, Jesus entered the Temple and began to drive out the people buying and selling animals for sacrifices. He knocked over the tables of the money changers and the chairs of those selling doves, and he stopped everyone from using the Temple as a marketplace. He said to them, "The Scriptures declare, 'My Temple will be called a house of prayer for all nations,' but you have turned it into a den of thieves."

Mark 11:15-17 NLT

The house of the Lord was never intended for, nor should it be used for, personal financial gains or taking advantage of others. It's a place where everyone should feel loved; where they can get help, prayer and encouragement. All the gimmicks, games, and things done for unrighteous gain, should be driven FAR away from the house of the Lord.

Ninety

He was with David when the Philistines gathered for battle at Pas-dammim and attacked the Israelites in a field full of barley. The Israelite army fled, but Eleazar and David held their ground in the middle of the field and beat back the Philistines. So the Lord saved them by giving them a great victory.

1 Chronicles 11:13-14 NLT

When king David reigned over the kingdom of Israel, he had thirty mighty warriors that supported and fought with him, along with the Israelite army. One of his top three men out of those thirty warriors was Eleazar. In this instance, Eleazar had David's back when the rest of the Israelite army ran and abandoned him. There may be times when you have lots of supporters, and other seasons when there's only a few faithful others fighting alongside and standing with you. Even if you have to face a trial alone, you can always encourage yourself in the Lord (look up 1 Samuel 30:6). Remember God is always with you and readily available. He is the one who will comfort, strengthen, and empower you to overcome and be victorious. Whether you have a million supporters, three hundred, one, or you're solo, you can depend on God, who cannot fail.

Ninety-one

Can two walk together, unless they are agreed?

Amos 3:3 NKJV

This verse touches on the importance of agreeing and being on the same page. A relationship can't have healthy growth with constant conflicting ways. For example, if you're married but only one of you is committed to doing things God's way, then there will be tension, confusion, stress and dissension. Married couples are considered one flesh (reference Genesis 2:24, Matthew 19:5, Mark 10:7-8, 1 Corinthians 6:16 and Ephesians 5:31), yet if the two are forcefully pulling in separate directions, they'll be torn apart. Physically speaking, ripped flesh or snapped joints are agonizing. When a godly relationship experiences breakage, it can be just as painful, exhausting and injurious. If you want healthily, promising, and productive relationships, then everyone involved must be in agreement on the overall goals and on who has the final say. God should be the one you seek for the first and final words when deciding the steps to take. The NLT version is written this way, "Can two people walk together without agreeing on the direction?" Let's agree to direct our attention to God and follow His way together.

Ninety-two

*And David became more and more powerful,
because the LORD God of Heaven's Armies was
with him. Then King Hiram of Tyre sent
messengers to David, along with cedar timber
and carpenters and stonemasons, and they built
David a palace. And David realized that the
LORD had confirmed him as king over Israel and
had blessed his kingdom for the sake of his
people Israel.*

2 Samuel 5:10-12 NLT

After David gets the word and is anointed by
Samuel (read 1 Samuel 16:1-13), he goes
through A LOT, before he officially becomes the
king of Israel. He had trials, struggles, physical
battles, personal issues, and much more. At this
point in the scriptures, he's already been king
and conquered more places. In verse 12 though,
it actually hits home: the word that God gave
him through Samuel -him becoming king- has

taken place. God's word is true, and He does not lie. What He reveals to us, more often than not, doesn't take place immediately or the next day. And yes, things can get worse before they get better. But regardless of what happens during the process, God's word and every promise He's made to you, will come true. Whether you see things lining up along the way or don't perceive them until after the fact, you can praise and give God His glory prior, during, and following, because His word is factual.

Ninety-three

In the seventh year of Jehu, Jehoash became king, and he reigned forty years in Jerusalem. His mother's name was Zibiah of Beersheba. Jehoash did what was right in the sight of the LORD all the days in which Jehoiada the priest instructed him.

II Kings 12:1-2 NKJV

Jehoash became king at the tender age of 7. He was blessed to have had a man of God in his life who instructed him in the things of God at such a young age. He wisely continued to follow that godly guidance as he matured and aged. If you weren't fortunate enough to have grown up with such guidance, it's never too late to get some. And if you're blessed enough to receive it, make sure to give back (share God's Word and precepts with other people, young and old.) Lastly, be sure to do like King Jehoash and follow it yourself.

Ninety-four

"Look," they told him, "you are now old, and your sons are not like you. Give us a king to judge us like all the other nations have."

1 Samuel 8:5 NLT

Samuel's sons weren't like him. They didn't have integrity or apply righteous judgment. They were greedy and took bribes. The people wanted them gone, and rightfully so. But instead of asking for God to bless them with some godly leaders, they desired and asked for a king. Basically, they wanted to be like the pagan nations around them. They were caught up in the world's ways and wanted what others had. They were rejecting God, foolishly thinking that something or someone else would be better. They would eventually get what they begged for. *"Do everything they say to you,"* the LORD replied, *"for they are rejecting me, not*

you. They don't want me to be their king any longer. Ever since I brought them from Egypt they have continually abandoned me and followed other gods. And now they are giving you the same treatment." 1 Samuel 8:7-8 NLT. Instead of influencing others to have what they had (the only true and living God as sole ruler and King), they had become influenced by people who didn't even know God. As children of God, we should be setting an example that others can and want to follow: Be like us, as we imitate Christ and not the other way around. Don't be like the children of Israel, who even when God warned them about what would happen if they had a king (like the ungodly people) and how bad he would treat them, still replied, *"Even so, we still want a king. We want to be like the nations around us. Our king will judge us and lead us into battle."*
1 Samuel 8:19-20 NLT

Ninety-five

Solomon tried to kill Jeroboam, but Jeroboam fled to Egypt, to Shishak the king, and stayed there until Solomon's death.

1 Kings 11:40 NIV

God told Solomon that He was going take the kingdom of Israel from his descendants (leaving them the kingdom of Judah) and give it to one of his servants. That servant turned out to be Jeroboam, a very capable and industrious young man, whom Solomon appointed officer over all the labor force of the house of Joseph (the tribes of Ephraim and Manasseh.) The Word of God doesn't stop people from opposing it, not even so-called people of God. People are prone to get in their flesh and try to prove God wrong (waste of time). We see examples of this through scriptures, from Saul trying to kill David, Solomon trying to kill Jeroboam, Ahab imprisoning Micaiah, and even King Herod trying to kill Jesus at birth. Not to mention numerous other occasions where people would be infuriated with God's people and prophets for simply relaying the true messages/word of God (perhaps this still happens today). I guess they failed to realize that no flesh or spiritual enemy can thwart the word of God or who He's anointed and called to do His will. If God has called or said He'll elevate someone, they WILL be promoted and exalted. No matter how much someone disdains the Word of God or what carefully designed plots they use against it, they will never stop it. The word will always accomplish what God sent it to do. In this case, when Solomon died, his son Rehoboam briefly reigned until Jeroboam returned from Egypt and assumed the position as king of Israel, just as God foretold.

Ninety-six

At that time the Spirit of the LORD will come powerfully upon you, and you will prophesy with them. You will be changed into a different person.

1 Samuel 10:6 NLT

Samuel is explaining to Saul what's going to happen, when God's spirit comes and abides in him. He'll be able to prophesy (speak the things of God) and change into a different person. The same is true when we accept Jesus as our Savior and allow Him to Lord over our lives. The power of the Holy Spirit will thrive (when we stop trying to restrict and control it), and we'll be transformed into true children of God. Then the things He's predestined and ordained for us, will start being fulfilled.

As Saul turned and started to leave, God gave him a new heart, and all Samuel's signs were fulfilled that day. 1 Samuel 10:9 NLT

Ninety-seven

Now all the people witnessed the thunderings,
the lightning flashes, the sound of the trumpet,
and the mountain smoking; and when the
people saw it, they trembled and stood afar off.
Then they said to Moses, "You speak with us,
and we will hear; but let not God speak with us,
lest we die." And Moses said to the people, "Do
not fear; for God has come to test you, and that
His fear may be before you, so that you may not
sin." So the people stood afar off, but Moses
drew near the thick darkness where God was.

Exodus 20:18-21 NKJV

They had the wrong idea about God, thinking
He was waiting to strike and kill them. They
didn't understand (although clearly, they should
have, since He hadn't struck them down for
their many rebellious and disobedient ways
along the way) that He was a loving, forgiving,

forbearing and compassionate God. A God that desires an affectionate relationship with His people. Yes, for our own good, we need to reverence Him. But we should never flee, hide or keep our distance because we're afraid. We're to be like Moses and draw nearer to God. Then we'll be able to experience and interact with Him, the way we're intended to.

Ninety-eight

Judah did evil in the eyes of the Lord. By the sins they committed they stirred up his jealous anger more than those who were before them had done. They also set up for themselves high places, sacred stones and Asherah poles on every high hill and under every spreading tree. There were even male shrine prostitutes in the land; the people engaged in all the detestable practices of the nations the Lord had driven out before the Israelites.

1 Kings 14:22-24 NIV

If you're familiar with the children of Israel and their delivery from Egypt in the book of Exodus, on to Joshua leading them and the periods detailed in the book of Judges, then you know how great and often their sins were. But now we see God's people, under King Rehoboam, has provoked God's jealous anger more than ANYONE before them. They'd basically become just like, if not worse than (because they knew better), all the enemies that God had delivered and protected them from. God's people always cried out to Him when they needed help or wanted deliverance from the surrounding evil nations but then would become just as evil or worse. Let's not copy their behavior. Don't become the very thing or worse than who or what you've previously asked God to deliver you from. He frees and sets us apart to live righteous and holy lives, not to get revenge or do whatever wicked and evil thing our flesh desires. You're better than that.

Ninety-Nine

Then he turned to Jehoshaphat and asked, "Will you join me in battle to recover Ramoth-gilead?" Jehoshaphat replied to the king of Israel, "Why, of course! You and I are as one. My troops are your troops, and my horses are your horses." Then Jehoshaphat added, "But first let's find out what the LORD says." So the king of Israel summoned the prophets, about 400 of them, and asked them, "Should I go to war against Ramoth-gilead, or should I hold back?" They all replied, "Yes, go right ahead! The Lord will give the king victory." But Jehoshaphat asked, "Is there not also a prophet of the LORD here? We should ask him the same question." The king of Israel replied to Jehoshaphat, "There is one more man who could consult the LORD for us, but I hate him. He never prophesies anything but trouble for me! His name is Micaiah son of Imlah." Jehoshaphat replied, "That's not the way a king should talk! Let's hear what he has to say."

1 Kings 22:4-8 NLT

King Ahab wanted King Jehoshaphat to help him
fight a battle. And although King Jehoshaphat
didn't mind helping, he was very wise in
wanting to seek God first. It's funny how, at
times, we refuse to seek God's wise advice
before we do something but won't hesitate to
fervently call on Him after that very thing has
blown up in our faces. Always seek God's truth
first AND follow His word/answer. If we're
truthful, there are certain occasions when we
already know the answer (as King Ahab did)
because of the scriptures and the Holy Spirit
giving us discernment. Just because you feel
God will say yes or no, doesn't mean you
shouldn't ask Him. Not seeking the truth won't
change or stop the outcome. Don't hate or
reject the person delivering God's word to you.
Also, avoid doing like Ahab and ask people who
lie and only tell you what you want to hear.
Four-hundred wrong answers you like, will

never be as good as the one truthful response you disagree with. And if someone were to ask you what God says about a situation, I hope you'll be as sincere as the prophet Micaiah was,

Meanwhile, the messenger who went to get Micaiah said to him, "Look, all the prophets are promising victory for the king. Be sure that you agree with them and promise success." But Micaiah replied, "As surely as the LORD lives, I will say only what the LORD tells me to say."
1 Kings 22:13-14 NLT

100

But be doers of the word, and not hearers only, deceiving yourselves.

James 1:22 NKJV

There was a lot of Word in this devotional. Hopefully you read it all, shared some, meditated on most, and even took notes. But above all, I pray that you'll be doers of the Word (allow the Holy Spirit to guide your actions) that you read, since "All Scripture is inspired by God and is useful to teach us what is true and to make us realize what is wrong in our lives. It corrects us when we are wrong and teaches us to do what is right. God uses it to prepare and equip his people to do every good work."
2 Timothy 3:16-17 NLT

I love you, but more importantly, God loves you beyond what you can fathom. I hope your relationship with Him expands uncontrollably and what He deposits on the inside of you explodes, affecting everyone you communicate or come in contact with. Glory to God!!!